SELF COACHING

Dr. Selim Ozdemir

UKEY Publishing
London-2020

Book : Self Coaching
Author : Dr. Selim Ozdemir
selim.tx@gmail.com
Editor : UKEY Team
Design : Ima Studio
Cover : Ima Studio
Publisher : UKEY Publishing
Series : Self Help 01
Version : V01
Copyright © 2020 Selim Ozdemir

All rights reserved. No part of this publication may be reproduced, distributed, or transmitted in any form or by any means, including photocopying, recording, or other electronic or mechanical methods, without the prior written permission of the publisher, except in the case of brief quotations embodied in critical reviews and certain other noncommercial uses permitted by copyright law. For permission requests, write to the publisher, addressed "Attention: Permissions Coordinator," at the address below.

http://ukey.let.in
ukey@ilet.in

SELF COACHING

Dr. Selim Ozdemir

Self Coaching

Index

THE PREFACE	5
About of Writer:	6
VISION CHALLENGE	**8**
MISSION CHALLENGE	8
VISION CHALLENGE	11
OL IZ VEL!	14
UNIVERSITY OF "UNITOPIA"!	17
WORKPLACE OF HOPE!	21
LIFE WITH EXCLAMATION!	24
THE PASSWORD OF LIVING TROUBLE	27
IS HUMAN SOURCE OR VALUE?	29
MORALE COACHING!	33
THE NEW ROUTE OF KAIZEN PASSENGER	35
INSTITUTIONAL SILENCE AND RIGOR MORTIS!	37
THE KEY OF PROBLEMATIC BUSINESS	40
WH QUESTIONS!	42
QUESTIONING ARTIFICIAL UNIVERSITIES!	45
THE VIRTUAL CHAT OF YEARS!	47
VIRTUAL CHAT WITH NEW YEAR!	52
INDIVIDUAL CHECK-UP	**55**
COACHING TO YOURSELF!	55
WHAT IS SELF-COACHING?	60
THE MEETING OF THE COACH WITH HIMSELF!	64
YOUR STYLE!	67
THE APPLICATION: COACHING PARAMETER	70
IT IS CONSCIOUSNESS MANAGEMENT, NOT LYNCH!	73

	Self Coaching
CONSUME THE BURNOUT SYNDROME!	76
YOUR INNER MOTIVATION SOURCES	78
YOUR SPIRITUAL INTELLIGENCE	81
YOUR COMMUNICATION ACCIDENTS	84
SELF-CONSCIOUSNESS PRACTICE	86
INDIVIDUAL SWOT PRACTICE	88
IDEAL SELF-COACHING	89
IDEAL COACH: YOURSELF	92

THE PREFACE

The Self-Coaching Book is the essence of our coaching sessions and workshops. The Art of Coaching (2016), The Coaching Practices (2019), and our Self-Coaching Book with the updated information have reached you by a top-down trip. The fiction of the book is based on a basis that is appropriate for the philosophy of the coaching profession. Since the fact that the coach did not know the answers beforehand, the starting point of a book that has been written over-coaching could not be different. We believe that the useable information given in the work related to coaching philosophy and applications will touch your life. The aim is to bring together the key parts of coaching by yourself.

The book consists of 2 parts;

A. Vision Challenge: We asked challenging questions that are based on coaching philosophy prudential vision-indexed, put interjections!

B. Individual Check-Up: We open up an opportunity to self-application by giving place to individual coaching check-up applications.

Thank you to all members of the "UKEY Publishing Family" who has laboured on showing up for the book. If this work can touch your life, this means that our book makes self-coaching and we become happy. In the hope of being helpful…

20.10.2020
England
Assoc. Prof. Dr. Selim OZDEMIR

About of Writer:

- Nearly 30 years of training, coaching, consulting, and publishing experience.
- The private education sector in Turkey between 1988-1993.
- 17 years outside of Turkey as a Business Administration lecturer.
- Short and long-term studies in nearly 20 countries.
- Guest university lecturer in Moldova between 1993-1995.
- Business Administration lecturer in Russia between 1995-1999.
- Business Administration lecturer in Azerbaijan between 1999-2009.
- The Director of Continuing Education Center in 2003-2004.
- The Director of MBA in 2006-2009.
- Business Administration lecturer in Turkey between 2009-2016.
- Established the MOTIVASPIRIN coaching virtual organization in the USA in 2011.
- The Entrepreneurship and Management Center Manager in 2012-2013.
- The Head of the Department of Business Management at different universities between 1995 and 2016.
- Freelance publishing consultant and coaching in Istanbul between 2016-2020.
- Established the UKEY Consulting & Publishing Ltd Company in London in 2020.
- Communicate in English, Turkish, Russian, Azerbaijani, and Gagauzi languages.

Author`s Books:
1. *"Stories"*, Ufuk-Istanbul, 2003.
2. *"Continuous Developing Way in Business and Private Life"*, Oscar-Baku, 2005.
3. *"Entrepreneurship Opportunities in Indonesia"*, Tita-Jakarta, 2010.
4. *"Family Businesses from Central Asia to Balkans"*, Nobel-Ankara, 2011.
5. *"Business Coaching"*, Cinius-Istanbul, 2016.
6. *"Coaching Practices"*, e-book, Motivaspirin-Istanbul, November-2019.
7. https://www.barnesandnoble.com/w/ko-luk-uygulamalari-selim-zdemir/1134208628
8. *"Living Writers Society"*, e-book, Motivaspirin-Istanbul, January-2020. https://play.google.com/books/reader?id=XfLKDwAAQBAJ&hl=en
9. *"Self-Coaching"*, e-book, UKEY-London, October-2020.

Self Coaching

A. VISION CHALLENGE

MISSION CHALLENGE

What about challenging yourself beforehand? What about writing a powerful mission story that will give a shock to you and your surroundings? If the following lines mean something different to you and wiggle something in yourself while reading, this means that your challenge trip is starting. How? Think and start, I will only make a convoy! Come on!

Milestones of self-coaching are; to understand yourself, to recognize your surroundings, to link up by adopting, and to take action.

You are in a challenge with yourself: You still have not found yourself in your aim of reaching yourself!

You are looking for a discovery that will discover you and keep you informed from you. How about discovering yourself?

You are experiencing a disappointment:

You had pride, dreams, problems but you did not dare to open up your suffering, your surroundings did not show any special effort. Oh, if only they could make a little self-sacrifice rather than a civil servant mentality, and give extra time to people who look like a closed box like you! It did not happen.

The one who does not know you, how does he know your trouble?

How can know the one who does not know your trouble? I am worried about you and I am not happy with this special and pretty beautiful life! I thought of the reasons for doing your job

Self Coaching

without love! I said, if the necessary guidance had been given to this person, he would not start to live that much pessimist.

In order to take revenge from your surroundings, do whatever you can in the name of leading them by struggling with each of your respondent's trouble. Even if you are a member of a lost generation, bring at least ten young to this society instead of you!

Be a lighthouse!

No matter which profession you are doing, every aspect of your life be a companion for every person all the time! Regardless of whoever the respondent is, give one-to-one counselling as much as you can at every opportunity in order to make them live a meaningful life. For all that, you have seen the negative part of the issue in society and you have learned what the positive should be! You owe a thank to your surrounding for that! Please, be spirits to your surroundings, be a mind, be a companion, be a sincere individual, and get over the formality! Give up on locking your door, when you open your door, please leave the lock of your heart running henceforward!

You!

Are you ready to support people who have been beaten in the lack of education to understand their identities, set meaningful goals, develop new learning strategies, take responsibility, put into practice by discovering internal motivation sources?

Looking Life with Querying!

How many times have you been a compass in solving the extraordinary problems of your respondents? Do you have any answers? Do not forget that the colour of the self-coaching hat is different from other hats: It does not have answers beforehand! It

Ukey.ilet.in
does not tender a ready solution! It tries to make a person find the solution by himself. Actually, it tries to make him find himself! It provides the "formation of awareness and alacrity!"

What do you want to do?

The answer to this question is hidden in you and your capacity! Self-coaching is, of course, indispensable but if you are not at peace with oneself, if you are not sympathetic and emphatic to your surrounding, you should not be shocked with dramatic and traumatic outcomes! Do you love life, people, and your profession? If your answer is not "yes" accurately, you can quit your profession! You may not have the courage that the person who says "You drained all your anger to your profession, please give my money back, I gave up from changing." Do not forget that; spoiling a life is not like changing money! Roosevelt says "If the character has not developed, the education does not work." Do not waste time with the things that will not develop your character, think over character education! The statement of your "I intend to self-coaching" is the password of the scenario new life version 'life 2.0'.

You seem to be ready to look at your own life with querying! From now on depends on your artistry! You continue to brainstorming, even if every seeker can not find it, those who find it is the seekers! If you start to exceed yourself, this means that it is time for you to take those who want and do not want to look at life with querying? Socrates says "If the story you're about to tell me isn't true, good or necessary, just forget it and don't bother me with it." in his triple filter test!

Be careful that the coaching you will do is true-well and convenient! In the life-game that has full of action, you are blown away as the pieces of the modern slavery system! You have to intend this skidding with the morality of rebellion to develop

Self Coaching
slowly but continuously and consciously without exaggeration, and to apply the positive change in all areas of life!

Ukey.ilet.in
VISION CHALLENGE

Every living is mortal!

Come, let's write the scenario together and the end of the movie will finish with a happy ending. You behaved bravely in your aim of reaching yourself! You discovered yourself! You buried the learned helplessness; from now on you have success stories! You are producing skill, not an excuse! Even if 'a skill is subject to a compliment', your philosophy becomes 'a compliment is subject to a skill!'

Since you have dip hope in your dream world, your ships have never sunk! When you love the created for the creator's sake, you have had so many synergy partners that you moved from the capital city of every day is a dream to the city of astonishment are niche nearly!

Before considering the realities, you searched yourself by questioning the strict idealist logic! When you feel depressed, you cheer up with the words 'there is no person without a problem!' You even did not reflect the moments that you were too sad and you cheered up people! Ignoring the fact that you are complaining about your workload, you said that "I love my trouble!"

You went out with positive energy every time you went out! When the moments that you start to lose your trust in yourself, you have become almost like having risen from ashes again! You got rid of your depression term and thrust out hand how many friends of you that have been tumbled down the hopelessness cliff! You started to understanding life in more differently! No longer that you love life so much that; you sometimes think that even you can be helpful to whole humanity!

Self Coaching

You aspired to be the madman of the tenth village, committed to being able to finish your life with a smile without pretending to be! The pursuit of this goal has become a vision challenge for you! You have had so many success stories that even will surprise you!

The skein of paradoxes! You live in such a world that there is exhaustion at the threshold of very quickly forgotten concepts! 'Total quality lessons' that are far from quality understanding, course attendees that have reading certificate who do not like reading, 'effective rhetoric workshops' that are far from effect, 'time management programs' that both the trainer and the participants stay late, intrafamilial communication experts tell the techniques that do not apply, 'applied for entrepreneurship courses' that there is no application... In these dilemmas and paradoxes chaos, although the understanding far from qualification, you tried to take a quality journey. This is a 'vision challenge.'

Students behave like studying, the educators behave like lecturing! Students behave like graduating, the institutions behave like giving diplomas! The graduates behave like searching for jobs; the businesses behave like giving jobs! The transactors behave like working, the businesses behave like paying salary... One of the last of the lifetimes that have passed as if doing a career; behaving as if being retired! Although, one day the door does not seem to be knocked on and does not pretend to take the incoming lives; it takes by remunerating for a job, quite qualified and without neglecting! This is the 'vision challenge!'

"Will management", "sustainable motivation", "time and conservation management" are the concepts that whose exterior is nice but the interior is empty with the contingency approach maybe! If you are saying 'I intend to pad these concepts' and if you are aspirant to being a helpful person with an unrestrainable wish; this is the "vision challenge" for you!

You did not even count how many people you helped for solving unusual problems. You became more modest when you wore the self-coaching hat and you moved away from the ego that is often seen in modern people! You experienced the excitement of not having the answers beforehand! You realized that you were not the deus ex machina that provides a ready solution! You reached to the solution by taking support but with your effort! You made talent scouter to yourself by using the tools of 'Awareness Management and Self-Motivation!'

The End of the Road Appears!

You entered from this door with the password of 'I intend to live qualified' and from now on, you are a character figurative who has devoted his life to humanity by exceeding yourself! You are aware that the conclusion is not your business and you are conscious that you need to give the right of this process! You know that every of your respondent can turn into a happiness wave in the world flood! You love and make self-coaching so that your own life and then the lives of those around you end with a smile; you don't pretend!

"The strategic intention" is the concrete equivalent of "what?"; "deep intention" is the abstract answer of "why"! The modern human that sings and plays like "I am done" with his profession/activity is afraid of diving into deep waters! Because being an aspirant underwater means breath control and "personality management!"

The Life that You Can Finish with a Smile!
Even though this mission is within the "adult" 's means, "how would you know?" is the last question, the last point of

Self Coaching

"every person's" repertory! However, before diving into the world of questions, the question of 'what is it, and what this mood is?' is the first point of awareness management! Here is the deep vision of the aspirant: "May God makes us human!"

OL IZ VEL!

When you wanted to study history, you found yourself in the Department of Business Administration, you faltered; at least, the talk of your teacher about the history of business provided you to hold onto the school. Since your memorizing is strong, you were very successful at test exams; you thought life like a multiple-choice exam as well! You felt yourself like a child whose toy had taken away in the open book exam system! How desperate you were! Was this a bad joke or the first signs of the conflict of your education life that you had taken years and your life?

Make a show off!

You were a child of a civil servant; he had very disciplined extremely meticulous and tough rules. 4 years finished quickly; you behaved like graduating- your university behaved like giving a diploma! You lived in a country that 'what you know is not important as much as who you know'; your father's friend who has a firm behaved like employing you by request! He gave a duty to me at the department of research and development by saying "I know the man from his eyes!" You started the job far from orientation like firm, sector, department, job description, business introduction! It is not 'Gangam Style'; this is how 'Turkish style' started a business. It is okay if the horse learned swimming at the sea if it sank, it was a job accident and no name. You behaved like working- they behaved like paying! On the one hand, you thought that you were working quite well but your performance did not recognize. Off to one side 360-degree performance assessment, the firm thermometer was showing – degree! You thought that 'It was in vain even if you made a bicycle kick in the coffin in this company!'

The Exam That the Corrects Took the Mistakes!

Self Coaching

The Management Coaching Workshop given by the company went beyond the ordinary! The educator had sections watched from 3 Idiots and made analyses. One of the most scenes you were most impressed with was the part that the job interview between company owners and the graduate student. When you were supposed to lose your hope, the statement in the movie that "Ol Iz Vel" came to your mind! You impressed a lot from movie readings of "Dead Poets Society" and "Every Child is Special" at the same workshop. You were pleased a lot at the end of the workshop when you heard that the achievement certificate exam would be tested! You would come round years later! When you took the exam paper, this was written on: In the exam, the mistakes do not affect the corrects; 5 corrects take 1 mistake!

Mission Examining...

You said "What am I doing?" by oneself and started to question your individual mission: You shouted out from inside "Do I have to live cross-eyed in the land of blind?" you wanted to cry! A storm was breaking inside you with rebellion morality by saying "How long could I work in this company where business blindness was thought true?" You grumbled by oneself "I must absorb the marrow of life before being fertilizer for worms! What will be my line in the world where the scene of strong' is exhibited? I must reveal my talents without having silent desperation."

You thought that 'I can't start life again, but I can start the remaining days with a new perspective.' You will continue playing with the anxiety of a work-food-wife or you will understand 'the day you live!' When were you going to say "Ol iz vel?" Did you do the things right? Did you do the right things? The questions had just begun to invade your brain that you flinched with your mother's voice "my baby you fell asleep, get up or else you will be late to the exam; you grew up but still watching the movie!"

Ukey.ilet.in

Firstly, you tried to understand what was going on wonderingly, and then you hug your mom tightly. You started to say "*Ol iz vel, ol iz vel, it will be mom, it will do not wonder!" You were crying. Your mom thought that you had seen a nightmare. However, you made your decision...

*The pronunciation form of "all is well" statement that passes in the Indian movie named as "3 Idiots".

Self Coaching
UNIVERSITY OF "UNITOPIA"!

Do you want to know the unusual University of Unitopia well?

Entrance without an exam! The practical program that the truth takes the mistake! Professional language instead of foreign language torture! Staff and assistant studentship! Participatory management! Registration and campus!

The admission to the University of Unitopia that you study will not be with the central examination! You will make a decision together by meeting with the department you thought! It will be 3 years if you want to study in formal 4-year faculties in research departments, 2 years if you want to study in practice departments, and 1 year if you want to study in Vocational Schools! If you are a successful faculty-student plus 1 or 2 years, if you are a vocational school student plus 1 year, you will receive a monthly scholarship from minimum fee by practicing in the places out of university! Your internship will be cancelled; you will be a paid company assistant in a contracting business!

Program

There will not be an education based on memorization! All of your exams will be electronic and the sources will be open! In the quiz exams, 4 true answers will take 1 mistake; the fallacy that a mistake takes a true answer will come to an end! Remote, virtual, online education programs will become a brand in Western Standard! All of your lessons will be broadcasted in a virtual place! You will not have a source problem in the University of Unitopia those bases on justice! The content of lessons and score system will be determined by the teacher and students like you commonly! The bullshit that compulsory optional subject will not be! As a student, you will have the right of choosing the lesson and teacher!

Ukey.ilet.in

Scholarship

Academic success will not be wanted by everyone! According to the talent management report and professional tendency list, talent scholarship like sport, art, etc. will be provided!

Foreign Language

The rate of foreign students will be %20 above the total number! There will be education with a foreign language except for international classes! There will be practical vocational language lessons distributed in equal hours to all education periods!

Students whose vocational language practice is not enough will not be able to graduate!

Academic Staff

The teacher will work with an annual contract! Academic appellations will be given according to performance examination by the relevant department and lectern! The CV of the teacher will be approved according to the lesson, research, social activity, trip abroad, and pupil-student that he has disciplined the number of journeyman-graduates! The teacher will not be able to enter lessons for more than 5 hours in a week! Monthly pays will be US standards on condition that producing the project, the charges will be funded from project incomes! Those who act contrary to the honor of the teacher will be given 5 hours of lecture hall and class cleaning weekly! Teachers will be asked to write 1 unique international article in a year! Participation support for foreign programs will be given! The duties of the teachers who have never been abroad will be temporarily suspended, they can continue their duties after going abroad for at least 1 year! Teachers who

Self Coaching

cannot use internet media effectively will undergo training with those who use it! Application department teachers will be required to have a start-up job! The teacher who does not produce at least 1 application-oriented project per year with his students will be dismissed!

Assistantship

As a student, you will be the partner of teacher companies with the logic of a labor-fund partnership! Every teacher will have at least 3 student-assistants! You will be paid hourly from the student assistant project budget based on minimum wage! Each department will have a career center! When you graduate, you will be a university partner and join the administration in exchange for leaving 5% of your earnings annually as a student development fund! The spendings like wedding expenses etc. of graduates will be sponsored by the fund!

Management

The warden will be selected among professional administrators whose projects have received the highest number of votes on social media, not by appointment! The university administration will be left to the common mind board! All head of departments and headships will be cancelled! A budget will be allocated to department and student clubs! Support service will be taken at the university by going to outsourcing based on volunteering from different professionals in the city! The caste system applications like staff, the student dining hall will come to an end! There will be only name-surname in offices, no appellations! There will not be follow-up factors like security, x-ray at the university entrance! The Municipality, Non-Governmental Organization, and students will provide auto-control on a voluntary basis!

Proposals

The following proposals will be presented to the center and will be the final decisions to be taken before abolishing itself:

-Making the necessary arrangements for leaving the university administrations to the professionals!
-Turning the faculties that have not career centers into high schools by closing them!
-Being managed all universities from its place by reaching to real sovereign texture!
-The announcement that The Higher Education Council does not exist since it will not be required!

Registrations are beginning!

Would you like to study at a university like that? Are you saying that took the biscuit, this is a utopia? This is not a utopia, this is Unitopia! Some of these are the applications that exist in advanced universities! Can it be applied at the universities that are balk at not to develop? Anyway, the ship does not sink in the dream world; whereas, many talents sink with the current bureaucratic education system! What will be lost if it is tried?

Campus

One day the future studies will finish; "The Campus of the University of Unitopia" will exist on the peak of "Mountain of Kaf", "Country of Niche"! We took the road towards that place! You are expected too! Are you coming?

Self Coaching
WORKPLACE OF HOPE!

Fuzuli suffers from the bureaucracy of the *Kanuni Period* in his *Indictment* and says that: "I saluted, they did not respond due to it was not a bribe!"

I said: Oh friends, this is the wrong thing, this is what sourness?They said: Our custom is like that!

I said: It is sin to use the good of the fund however you want!

They said: We has bought it with our coin, it is halal for us!

I said: If they take into account, the depravement of the way your support is found!

They said: This account is asked at the end of the world!

I said: The account exists even in the world!

They said: We do not have fear even from it, we have persuaded clerks!

I recognize that they do not give an object different than an answer; I have left the challenge desperately and walked away.

The distance that extends to polished ego era, the phone that rings busy all the time, hello with an appointment, talent without compliment-clumsy compliment, breath that can not exceed its personality, stream without the pearl, castle without flag, the mother who does not cry, the one who stays late to his wedding, finds the death early, lips without greeting, prayer without prayer, a little friend that worries about fleece, a worm that gnaws the system silly, excuse without talent, the one who falls for a lie, the pine that tumbles down, the relative that cracks up, the door that is closed and what next!

You said that the doors are sliding, you cut shroud to the one who does not think like you! You achieved adding kilometers, hung locks to common places! You approached prejudiced even to hello, you said that this was a bribe and did not respond! You exaggerated the issue too much that, even the comer was the grim reaper, you swore that you were busy! It was already your own person, he could not have a value; it was you who said: "There will be not an ox from house calf!" As a member of a generation that made a wound, closed a door, you embarrassed your ancestors who opened an age and closed an age! A friend is a life to a voice, to a longing, could not run to you with bated breath! So, while there was gurgling together at the flow of the water that was named as life, swallow stayed to the destiny of a lonely one! He swallowed and forgot! Was the forgotten one is you or him?

Neither the door left, neither the bridge! The closed-door, the collapsed bridge, the dried creek that can not gurgle at the flow of the water that was named as life, half-liver that gave up from being a liver! The hasty person that sends an invitation to enormity like wanting well-being! The tired who turns into chasing behind livelihood "everything" without being aware of the livelihood that is hung on his neck! The one who does not get tired from rubbing salt in the wound, drawing "good" to mistakes! Kamikaze, who sees animosity less to mind, starts to hate to live! The poor who is exhausted from being misunderstood or not being understood!

Listen to the call of the workplace of hope: Hey best friend! "Pain; when it stings to your soul like a thorn when the anger runs like a steed, sadness, when falls over you like a tree, you will stop," you will take a deep breath thinking hope flowers. "When you lost at the nameless seas like an adventurous seaman, you will think that the land will be seen one day. You will dream the voice

Self Coaching

that 'The land is seen!' The land, even it has never seen, at least you will know that what you are looking for and what you have lost! You will understand that all the storms that you have experienced have gained a mean with that hopeful aim that you hope you will arrive. Even if you lose everything, you will not lose your dreams. You will never forget what you are looking for. The more you remember your joys, the more you understand the depth of pain. While the darkness is coming down, you will look to the light more carefully. When they put a cliff that monsters walk around at your's foot between you and yourself, before leaping that you do not know how to end, you will take power by remembering your past, your joys, your dreams."

Persisting in crazy waters that demolish bridges, you will build bridges and open doors. You will think of the crocodile that cries after eating his children, you will not care the inexperienced dealing, and you will bury the pain, the anger, the sadness to Kaf Mountain in your heart on the brink of not reviving again. You will say "No matter what comes to spirit, whether rigour or enjoyment, both of them are a pleasure to spirit, either its favour or distress is pleasant." Even they want your life, you will go without looking your back by saying "all right" like laughing to going to darling with a sweet song on your mouth.

Pandora's Box was opened and the evil spread around! The sound that came from the box 'please take me out, only I can cope with the evil' drew attention, and the box was opened for the last time! It was the hope butterfly that got out of the box! It started to flap across to all evil! It flew, flew, and flew since putting all evil to the box again! Because it was hope! It forgot all the evil! This call is to you! Are you ready to fly?

LIFE WITH EXCLAMATION!

It has become easier for you to look neatly with a little effort in the irregular piles! The concept 'Time Management' is rebelling to modern people! Would it attract your interest if we offer the concept of 'Time Management'? To give up from the aim of being organized in the army of irregulars was keeping the mind busy, an incomparable compliment came to the rescue! After all, everybody needs to 'well done!'

Dearie every day is important and a reinvigoration! The most important day is the one that is fruitful and unusual the song of reinvigoration is sing! I wish you examined your day at the end of the day and actually yourself! I do not say that keep watching me and be my follower; the important thing is not tagging behind me, I say the important thing is you're staying with me! In fact, rather than reaching people, the aim of human's reaching oneself looks like more valuable! You still could not reach yourself; you are looking for an explorer that will discover you and keep you informed of you!

Oh, your these learned despairs! The alternative treatment is to make skill management, not excuse! If you act in accordance with the theory of unexpectedness, it will be possible to give more meaning to life with short passes in the confined space! However, while your mind is doing belly dance with chaos in the skein of expectations, how can I tell you about this?

It makes sense to continue way with dreams; especially if you can add hope to the dreams, it will be very enjoyable to knock the door of astonishments position with the synergy that will occur! When 'the dreams reach to the land of Niche from the capital city', you have to be ready for the mood of the silence of dream by eluding from the mood of unusual lines!

Self Coaching

In the name of turning the world life that consists of a game to a more meaningful situation, you have to evolve to being a proactive person instead of being a passive person; but, for this, strategic intention necessarily! If your brain sends an early warning signal to your intention of evolving from the position of "audience" to role of "performer" by surprising, this means that your incubation term has not finished, you should not hurry, you are in the term of "active patience" now!

In this life, 'spare person' is found every time, but 'engine person' is not found every time! The team players without however are the absolute must of team spirit! "Oh team spirit, if you have come, knock our heart door 3 times"

"They say a matter of life or death but my eyes are on the die! Life has missing, life is missing in life! I wish I had wear wings; was a bird and raced! Persisting in the quite empty motherland, I wish I went to Matan!" Life or die is more serious than being taken seriously, that's why "even being afraid is not enough, shaking is necessary!"

The situations of "Sizzling frequency" are witnessed a good many! If we open in the format of "The lack of perception that is seen in unstable people", can it be understood? These sizzling situations made "writer" the distressed ones! However, it is more enjoyable to "kill" people's heart! Beyond all of them, writing is easy, living is hard!

"Will management", "sustainable motivation", "time and conservation management" are the concepts that are maybe all fur coat and no knickers but with the contingency approach! If you say 'I intend to fulfil the inner of these concepts' if you are aspirant to being a helpful person with an unrestrainable wish; the word

Ukey.ilet.in

"who requested and was serious in his request, he found" has to be your milestone!

No matter how original you think in the boundaries of your village; If your horizon is not wide, the things that you can do are as far as the boundaries of your village! In fact, the mad of each village is the exchanger leader for this reason! 'Continuous development travel' will not finish even with the last breath; 'continuous astonishment travel' will appear on the horizon! When it comes to physical roads, it is worth staying sleepless for the end!

There is no 'The delegation of authority' in the act of thinking! The master says "go wherever your heart takes you!" The word "I indent to being an apprentice and finding a master" is the first step in the name of being an apprentice! The rest is artistry and destiny thing! Your destiny finds you; you look for the peace! Put the exclamation in your life and look for yourself!

THE PASSWORD OF LIVING TROUBLE

Isn't it strange that adding immortal meanings to the things you fictionalized as a mortal who will born-grow up-die? 'You build-your child protected-your grandchild studied the history of business', it burned-ended and burned away! An important question for self-accounting: "Did you left a nice sound at the canopy?" While there is being a nice sound; do not waste your lifetime as empty enjoyment-run rigour! As Akif said: "It is a big life lost!" As a Y generation, here is the language you will understand: "The years have passed in vain!"

I guess it is best to close all associations and gather all institutions under the roof of "Dead Poets Association!" However, the others are singing-you are playing; at least you play appropriate for your mission, you do not do outsourcing for heart cleaning!

What was the Coach saying to bards of association: "Let's understand the day we live by making the life extraordinary, we need to collect the buds while there is time; because one day all of us will be a forage to worms!" Since the words-ideas can change the world, it is necessary not to experience silent desperation and to scream silently by feeding with the rebellion ethics to the troubles!

While the scene of the strong continues in the world; I wonder what will become of your line: Troubled life?/ Responsible life? It is useful to listen to the questions before the interrogation session! A profitable life? / Modesty life? The profit without modesty is not a profit!

Ukey.ilet.in

I say; whatever you have fiction will end anyway! Rigor Mortis will knock on the door anyway! For a pleasant voice and a qualified air; rip off your infertile life plaque; hang this one: I am moving! From troubled life > to responsible life!

If you are tired from looking for a solution to similar problems with similar methods; if you think institutionalization is necessary and you cannot get rid of being situative; if you want to evaluate people as value, not a source; if you target the management of awareness against environmental threats and opportunities; if you desire to make idea gymnastic with modern management applications; if you open your heart to brainstorm on the harbour of leadership-motivation; if you say "I intend to an active life!"; this means that you have started to the searching conference!

If you say! I don't know what I have been looking for!', since you cannot go back to the first years of your career, go to the first sentence of the article! Do not waste your life far from awareness management, empty pleasure-run rigour! Examine your intention and join `Living Poets Society`! "It is for the remarker, remarker, what is for the blind, what is blind?" Give up from looking, try to see! If you say I intend to live a peaceful and cautious life, enter the password: "……."

Self Coaching
IS HUMAN SOURCE OR VALUE?

"Yesterday went with yesterday my dear, it is necessary to say new things," Mawlana called you centuries ago. While repeating this word often, you are not aware that you are not saying a new thing! However, even "telling new things" is not enough anymore; "you need to do new things!" It is necessary to write new things! We have said human sources, it has not! We have said Human Values, the human has not a name, has not worked! Doomsday Management from now on!

Social Tailoring!

Your problem is not a lack of information, it is a lack of application. You have to display the morality of rebellion in the style of "That much information is enough for me, allow me to experience what I have learned" in the knowledge chaos that has been thrown down your head. There is a lot of necessity that your social tailoring, idea labour that will mean dress to the concepts that stay without garment!

Despite Western Societies that produce and consume a lot, it is time to get out of dual life as a member of Eastern Society that produces little-consume a lot with meaningless skiddings. Start from yourself to purifying and simple life. Do not neglect to turn your face to positive energy sources in order to stay young in the old world where compulsory transformations are experienced and swept from crisis to crisis. Take a journey of development, get out of your career concerns, and start a self-confidence transfer!

You have come to the end of the swirling and meaningless change stories with the concepts you emptied. It is not a change, it is continuous development that the concept you actually need. Rather than quality management applications that have not to spirit, what really matters is ethic management. It is not 'human sources management', even it is not 'human values management' too, there should be another concept together with the individuals that cannot melt their ego in the pool of common mind!

Breaking the memorialization should be your basic mission. While you are sitting hot chair of state, you cannot make a 'self-sacrifice' call to the cold. Sign up for the empathy seminar right now! The essential is the values like team spirit with common mind-directed, the exciting dream, business ethics based on sincerity, work-sharing applications that accept people at their position, time collocation that is an elixir of unsystematic. Tolerate them.

Not telling the wrong is sedition! Do not attribute holiness in itself to institutions that consist of stone and cement. The expression of your "I do not want any criticism to my institution" is actually the case of telling the indistinction of 'I do not want any criticism to the institution that I cannot handle well' in a manner. The systems are for humans; you should certainly examine the pitiless systems that do not produce peace and the applications that are not humanistic for 'the most honourable human'. Do not forget, keeping quiet is sedition, not telling the wrong! Examining the human that examines systems is what a big standoff, paradox, dilemma. The circle of your that criticize your method and procedure actually wants to make you a favour like 'smacking to the scorpion on your shoulders'. As your ego swells, you start to not caring the scorpion on your shoulders. Your administrative privilege depends on your administrative skill. If your administrative skill is insufficient, you often roll to value chaos. Look to get up quickly! Deciding on your own without having sufficient experience in your position means; seducing the collective spirit, dynamiting our awareness, and sending the common mind on a holiday. Your idea of 'Only I know' makes the devil singing belly dance music, don't you see?

Even if it does not take a place as a part of the administration books, 'poetic justice' is one of the important topics of life book! Here is an administration-accounting from that life book: Do not say I know everything, you will not open a door without a collective movement key, you do not think of yourself as "genius", you will see your surroundings as a human before!

You do not eat even rice without a plan, you will say *"we're going to see this thing through, come hell or high water"* after starting an action.

You will take your head between your hands and say *"what am I and what is this situation?"*

You know the differences between the organization and human organism, you will know the ways beforehand in order to direct people, you will not see human sources as a source machine, you could say "What does money matter, the important thing is human values!" The ego of human as you will accept as a value, you will actualize institutive talent management by ensuring dissolve its ego in the collective pool!

You will say"The one who is motivated by fear makes something due to necessity, the one who is motivated by a sense of duty makes something due to he has to do, but the one who is motivated by his spirit makes something due to he wants", you will not forget spiritual intelligence and will not make them sleep!

"Oh dear!" you will not control people, the actual thing is the business follow-up; you will not see your workers as 'sheep', You will not forget that you are a shepherd, you will shake by thinking the right of the ones whom you cannot motivate!

Ukey.ilet.in

Look, there is a horse far away, whether you go or ride, that horse is our horse! You will not take power from your armchair; you add power to your position, the armchair resembles the horse, you will know that!

Is your mind wrapped up in the horse? You will say 'What a beautiful horse to ride for running away from management.' One early morning, you will go to the irreversible places by riding that horse, "The death is a festival for the dead, here is rejoicing to the festival. Oh, how nice, there is riding a wooden horse at the festival." You will not forget!

MORALE COACHING!

The 3 main headings of Drucker's management workshops are; (1) focus on the strengths (2) talent selection, (3) management of opportunities. Instead of the pushing questions to black-white tones like is it true or wrong, you need to begin a quest that can be appropriate to your necessities from the point of the content of this idea needs comment! Your remedy has been summarized in these 3 items: Especially pay attention to the item 2! Although, in order to the exploration of your talent you beforehand should say "I intend to the exploration of my talents!" If you can't do this talent exploration, one day, "we know him/her well but he/she is insufficient" might be said after you.

The concepts that take place in Western literature arose as a response to a problem in social life, not as a fantasy. The difference of the Eastern Societies that you are a member of becomes clear at that point: Neither those problems are your problems nor those concepts are your concepts! How much correct is it to attempt to apply their solutions directly to your problems? Haven't we chosen the expressions "self" and "challenge" just because they seem more valuable to you? When will you realize that you cannot be as systematic as Western people and but a Western human also cannot have a practical intelligence that is particular for the East people? When you activate the subtle wit that you use everywhere at this point, the western concepts will cease being a fantasy one by one from your world, start to appearing literally. Look, the sun always rises from the east! Its setting is from the western! Only one day the sun will rise from the west and go down from the east; that will be the value of humanity! I say that every day you make the sun birth from the western, put an end to the cunning of the sunk from the east, and do not experience little dooms every day!

Ukey.ilet.in

Is there a moral embarkation centre that listens to humans' troubles in your workplace, shares grief with their troubles, helps to produce a solution with the applications rather in a different style from classic method perceptive and cliché motivation tools in your environment? If your answer is Human Resources give up; I have changed its name to the story! The response of the management of human resources is a story both for micro-level businesses and macro-level ones! Let alone human resources, we've disburdened even the concept of human values in a short time! What about morale coaching instead of sigh management? You will be the moral source of your environment on a voluntary basis. If you say I am a volunteer, this means you will do with your acquiescence, not with money. Because you will be serving as a morale coach, not the one that is serviced! You will be the talent midwife as a morale coach, not its gravedigger! It's the high time of the question that demoralizes the directors: Boss boss boss?

It is not enough to change the concepts, the appellations only on the business card, a conscious catharsis is necessary by intending to change your mentality! Because fishes stink beforehand, horses neigh according to their owners!

Self Coaching
THE NEW ROUTE OF KAIZEN PASSENGER

The human history is actually on a development journey covered with inventions! The country that invented zero (0) is India. Do not underrate saying that it is zero, if it hadn't been, we could not go to space! You, who invented the space, unfortunately, could not discover yourself! You've learned going to the moon but you are learning washing your hands only just! I guess, the day you reset yourself, not your human, your spirit will get on to the space shuttle and fly to the dreams country of Kaf Mountain in order to the build of your peace throne!

If you will not be the visioner person that breaks ground, the word of hope will be erased from your dictionary! If you can be a little aware of your talents, you will have been got rid to the infertility of vision. Give it up looking for medicine now, you are the remedy of your problem too. Think about how you can prompt the talent factory that you will make amazing discoveries belong to you!

When the books of some old writers were stacked on top of each other and calculated, including childhood, 15-20 pages of writing accrue to each day of a whole life! This must be the management of fertility! Although you get along as being literate! Your writing ability is almost trapped in the Twitter world limited to 280 characters! The more you spin, the more you spin! The easy and virtual version of the charity race! Though be careful; as the number of your shots increases, you can see yourself as a native member of Megalomania Shooters Club!

As for reading... 'Have you said fast and effective reading?'. Pass! Repeat; social media has been invented, bravery has been destroyed! Do not understand reading as 'sorting people

Ukey.ilet.in

out'! May God not leave anyone without a book! As an untutored expert, you are persistently still telling the Kaizen Philosophy and the story of quality! It must be asked: If you have Kaizen in your life philosophy, why is there no development in your life philosophy? If you understand and tell continuous improvement as continuous education, I have to send you to unpaid time off!

Actually, one time you have told me that "I hate the people that say yes sir to everything around me, I want to be told the truth from my around; whatever it takes!" The ones that you have told this have confirmed you by shaking their's heads and you have become happy! You continue to diverting yourself as 'successful'; when the day comes that the ones who are compelled to you wriggle from job-food-wife concern, who knows what will they say? Oh, that you learned despairs! Read the banana bunch in the cage and "5 monkeys" narrative and break your locks!

While you are making a plan, your destiny is smiling! Start overdrawing your career map and renew the route of development journey! Do not forget; you are not desperate, because you are the remedy! May your fate be without sadness, your career without a barrier! With the philosophy of 'break to excuses, hello to skills' you have said 'I intend going to a development journey', right? Do not look to see if anyone is coming! Open the bounce and take the road! May godspeed you!

Self Coaching
INSTITUTIONAL SILENCE AND RIGOR MORTIS!

Think of an institution; an organization that grows and develops with the right decisions and applications increases its trust with every success it achieves and develops its success potential when its self-confidence increases! However, while a healthy development of the leader's communication with his team and his environment is expected in proportion to the development of the institution, continuous success may drag the senior management away from this understanding! If you do not take precautions for squint in the management, this can turn into administrator blindness! Welcome to the beginning station of the vicious cycle!

The concept of entropy has a negative meaning in Management Science. It refers to the tendency of energy burnout in the system, disruption in activities, balance disorder, increase in confusion and eventually the stop of activities of the system. We can summarize entropy as the loss of dynamism, flexibility, and communication ability of the organization. If you can start studies in the name of tackling the stability, entropy will leave its place to 'negative entropy'. As entropy evolves to negative, the positive transformation journey in the institution will continue.

In order to tackle the entropy, you should definitely mention the works that are not done in accordance with the institution mission and vision. If the management stage has closed this door intemperately, "institutional silence' mood starts! Sending institutional justice to unpaid time off is like writing an invitation to poetic justice; no joke! If only each denomination had a sturdy ombudsman, every person had a cautionary! The only mission of the ombudsman centre; It should be the sake of the

Right, not the creature! The duty of a positive auditor is; to say true as a god!

'Rigor Mortis' will be the point that the persistence of continuing on the road ignoring entropy will throw the institution! Since Rigor Mortis is a road of no return, you can suggest two alternative roads to your environment before entering that road:

Restructuring

In order to make your institution effective again, you should systematically review the existing structure, and reflect whatever denomination-decision-application that needs to be removed-added from the organization chart. Green light...

Change Engineering

If your previous application has not been enough, if you have applied it untruly or if you have not done it at all, your last remedy will be to make radical changes instead of minor improvements in your institution. You should renew all processes from top to bottom, and design your organization from scratch. Yellow light...

Rigor Mortis

If you have neglected change engineering too, your institution will inevitably roll into the cliff with continuous alarm bells! As a result of the institutional abduction of reason, Rigor Mortis is at your door! Rigor Mortis is 'hardness of death'! The hardness of death is the end of the road, the beginning of the end! Yes, "each mortal will taste the death"; institutions born-grow-die like people! Although, you should get prepared consciously for the moment "how would you know?" The actual issue must be 'to

Self Coaching

leave a pleasant sound in the canopy' after 'the coffin rest that is a prayer rug sultanate'! Red light...

The poet says: "The lover says that do not be offended from the one who hurts you. Because this world is a land of resisting, not resentment! Do not look for the ease in this world, do not be an aspirant to the ease! Since every taste has been tortured, the old world cries occasionally! Yahya Kemal has not screamed in vain in his Silent Ship: "Since many of those who go are glad about their's place that many years have passed; there is no turning from their's expedition!"

May all your efforts before Rigor Mortis be for a 'pleasant sound!' Since the world has not even left for Sultan Suleiman, you have to intend to play your role on the world stage without neglecting it! Have the intention that you can smile despite Rigor Mortis when they intend for you! You are at the last stop of the Vision Challenge journey. It is time to set out on a different and endless journey with a smile!

THE KEY OF PROBLEMATIC BUSINESS

If you say that 'I intend to evolve from problematic to responsibility and to be a part of a solution, not the problem', heed my words: Destiny finds human, although human should look for the peace; 'even it is not found by searching, the one who has found is the searchers!'

Do not say 'It has been a good word!'; because writing is easy, living is hard! You try to live what you have read and made live what you have lived! Throw the N, open a door to M; throw being problematic, look for being responsible! As a prudent business person, heed to problems, open your doors to responsible business... Do not look for the key, where it is in this article!

A person is born, grows, and dies! Beneficence remains from humans; whatever he has left in the name of goodness and beauty! You start a business, it develops and dies! Memories remain from your business; 'you start, your child protects, your grandchild studies business history!' The actual thing for human and organization, 'to leave a pleasant sound in the canopy' nearly! The ones who have come for enjoying oneself, because the ones who have been the sound leave a mark! 'The study of thinking about how to leave a mark behind you' is actually every of your day!

Let beneficence, knowledge, fairness live so that humanity lives! Let subversion, favouritism, draft kill so that your business lives! Do you have the mission to understand the vision sentence "Let the human live so that the state lives!"? "Where is this going" with your clumsiness that actually neglects yourself and makes nearly doormat whatever belongs to the values atlas, sees the customer like a haunt, only runs behind impudent profit? What a

Self Coaching

big paradox that you are declaring social responsibility projects without giving value and neglecting the individuals around you! Where are you the sincerity management?

What stage are you in reacting to the social demands: Are you obliged? Are you a volunteer? Are you conscious? If you neglect those, your business has reached the last stage, be aware: You cannot recall the business spirit with reorganization or change engineering sessions! It is too late for the question "What am I and what is this situation?" Rigor Mortis's hello, the last minute of the business!

Are you responsible? Are you problematic? What is your responsibility strategy? Reactive? Proactive? Defence? Harmony? I have said "The harmony; is not sleeping, I have adapted to the crowd is not at all; you have said 'It has been a nice word'! When the collective consciousness, team spirit, common mind goes on a holiday; the invitations like "to live only and freely like a tree and like a forest by brotherly, this longing is ours" stay on the lines.

Is it absolute that tumble down your business in order to evolve from problematic business to responsible business? "What kind of a world this world is its story is hard; its place is a surface, its time is suspicion; all the universe is décor; the whole humanity is surrender to lie!" Here is the companies accounting.

WH QUESTIONS!

You hear the concept of WH Questions! It states the essential questions that constitute the elements of the news: "What? When? Where? How? Why? Who?" If these elements are missing in a news, that news is accepted as insufficient. Nowadays, I have smiled when I learned that it is used as "6WH Questions" by adding the question "From Where?" to these elements in communication faculties. Since a ship will not sink in the dream world and the cost of a dream is zero –except the time cost of light pink dreams- it is worth exploring!

Have a private meeting with yourself at the first opportunity! Think about the concept of WH Questions and make an idea gymnastic. Are WH Questions enough in the name of formulating an active life? You can code swiftly with keywords like the what question as to the activity when the question as a process, where the question as to place, how question as factors, why question as general/private aims, who question as entrepreneur/boss/manager and try to think their expansions.

When we look at the question of why especially for commercial foundations from the perspective of general purposes; We can state the general purposes like (1) making a profit, (2) providing social benefit, (3) sustainable business, and (4) …!

What would you say if I asked you what item 4 could be? You can't find it, right? If you find, write here and share it with me too! This concept, whose social responsibility is not visible, even though it is well known has not come to your mind, right? The curiosities hit the top when I say this concept, which whom I asked cannot find, actually have an atom effect in increasing the profit, but they neglected this concept since they only focused on the profit and did not keep their docket busy enough, however an

Self Coaching

answer still cannot be found. I guess you are in the same situation! Since you have neglected him, the one you search and he neglects you too!

The fourth –indispensable- I leave you with your seeking meetings with yourself by not telling what is the purpose and close this chapter! Let me give you a hint: "Impudent profit is not a profit!" Come on, one more hint: I believe that one more wh question should be added to the wh questions! Businesses need to a basic wh question that will come before the other wh questions as much as air and water! Like Sultan III. Murad says "this world is mortal, do not fall for it, do not stand to the crown being haughty, do not rely on by saying seven climates are mine, wake up oh my eyes from the inattention wake up, wake up my sleepy eyes wake up" I want to say 'wake up!' I guess it is time to intend on thinking "……" factor that should be the first wh question!

Your actions are according to Wh questions! If the wh question no is (positive), the result can also be no(soundness)! If the wh no is negative, then there will be no good sign of your fate! You need to strategic wh questions, vision or aim, mission, or awareness management about consçsous duty understanding! I think that one of the main titles of the Fertility Management section that is not included in the management books should be "….." and it should take place before the planning that is accepted as the first of 4 management function! Do not say that the strategic plan has already been on the literature; I'm saying something beyond it and in a different dimension! Try to forget all my sayings right here! I guess it is time; you should intend to write your own life story with the concepts from you that will address your own world! This has become like a 'mission challenge' and it is not bad!

Welcome to the market of contrasts! Determination of needs, not demands; personality management, not perception;

inner motivation, not external; morale management, not staff; fertility economy, not wastage; deep vision, not strategic plan, story, not iky; poetic justice, not organisational, collective talent, not self-confidence; theory of non-expectation, not an expectation, living like at the winter of life, not 'as if!' The hard thing is not writing or reading; absolutely living! First of all "…..!"

Self Coaching

QUESTIONING ARTIFICIAL UNIVERSITIES!

Paradox: "Let ten servant wait for ten stamps of God; Full nine to one person, a stamp to nine people. Even if the wolves would be the king to the sheep, they would not do this slash; Hooray, black-market the guarantor of my cerement!"

Detection 1: Despite the whole wealth, humanity lives the poorest period of its history maybe!

Example 1. Location: Indonesia-Aceh Island. The fact that people have the right to buy fuel above a certain limit per day, even though the Aceh is found above the petrol-golden-natural gas reserves!

Question 1: Who will remind intellectuals (!), especially economists, that resources are not insufficient and that the actual problem is unfair distribution? It is a pity!

Detection 2: Despite the whole sociocultural historic dynamics, humanity perhaps lives the most unethical era of its history.

Example 2: The tragicomic events that have been lived in the public institutes behind the Kaf Mountain!

Question 2: When will the artificial university officials give up pretending to teach even the Business Ethics Lessons with inappropriate methods to ethic? It is a shame!

Detection 3: Despite the all practice ability, humanity is experiencing perhaps the most memorizing period of its history!

Ukey.ilet.in

Example 3: There are students who cannot express themselves in the exams based on open-source interpretation applied in all undergraduate-graduate courses, who do not have a dream beyond the cliché, and even demand that the exams should be done with based on memorization test easiness!

Question 3: When will artificial university officials give up making students memorized what they have memorized? It is wastage!

Detection 4: The qualifiers tell the quality ornerily and do not live qualified, even tell the ethic with the unethical methods and do not work in accordance with business ethic; pretend like living the starch.

Example 4: Look here the artificial university lessons!

Question 4: "The mirror of a person is work, do not be looked to the word!" When and why Ziya Pasha used this statement and what has been changed in the dark world of the intelligentsia? The lifetime is finishing!

Each of the 4 questions is 25 points. Duration: 1 lifetime!

The rights take the wrongs, not the wrongs take the rights!

If you want to be successful, consider your intention first!

Your motivation word will be this, it comes good: Thank God that there are people whose ideas are deep and hearts are honest, the things are going in someway nevertheless! What if you also put your hands under the stone more consciously!

Self Coaching
THE VIRTUAL CHAT OF YEARS!

New Year (NY): Are you going?
Old Year (OY): Yes, it is time to go!

NY: Are you going just because I have come?
OY: Don't you come because I'm leaving?

NY: Let this come-go game and stay with us!
OY: I have to go since the time given to time has finished!

NY: How long have you lived?
OY: 365 days! I am tired, not old!

NY: It would be great if you stayed and I took the advantage of your experiences.
OY: It is a relay race… Have you ever seen the same team athletes running side by side in a relay race?

NY: I have seen it! They run side by side when they win!
OY: I am the boiler, you are the ladle, let's try hopelessly. "Wanting the impossible is impossible!"

NY: Did you say something like "Never say never"?
OY: Do not use the word "Never say never!" to me *never*!

NY: Okay *never*!
OY: I wanted to say "Wanting the impossible is impossible."

NY: Is it costly to want, my dear; why it would be impossible? There is no impossible, just it takes a little bit of time! It becomes like honey!
OY: It would be like poisonous honey!

Ukey.ilet.in
NY: I "doesn't" understand!
OY: Leave the grammar! Look kid, you are too callow yet! I am already dolorous; let my opportunity that I spend my last hours without stress, okay?

NY: What is it, fear of death?
OY: No dear "the one who thinks its end cannot be a hero!" Although the one who does not think its end cannot have a thinker!

NY: You say "I think, therefore I am!"
OY: I say 'I am thinking, so hit me then!'

NY: I did not know that word like that!
OY: You learn by living what a great crime is thinking!

NY: As you started to philosophize, I have become afraid to think!

OY: "Think, do not fall! You fell, do not think!" (A graffiti of a prison!)

NY: Are you saying do not be too to think, or do not think?
OY: I think my time has become narrow rather good and I am melting, men. I will answer this question from social media then!

NY: People are very curious about what kind of a year I will be!
OY: What is there to wonder; you will be one of the 4,5 billion years past! The more people wonder about the external world, how much they neglect their inner world!

NY: How do you know they neglect?
OY: I know people very well.

NY: Don't you act unfairly by behaving prejudiced?
OY: It is better than summary execution! Besides, mine is not prejudiced; it is the last judgement!

Self Coaching

NY: Do not say "no law"! You cannot reach to the last judgement before consuming the inner law or appeal!
OY: No law? Burnout syndrome of the law! You go before it comes, look!

NY: Where?
OY: Whatever, you learn by living! Achoo!

NY: God bless you!
OY: It is not "God bless you", it is "Live freely!"

NY: This is the first time I've heard to sneeze "live freely" said!
OY: I have struggled a lot in order to change the wrong things that are an obstacle to living freely. Although people have turned out more stubborn than me.

NY: So you couldn't change them?
OY: I have changed but couldn't improve! Maybe they are not aware but I have aged all of them one more year. But, I could not afford my power and time to erase many taboos, behaviour deviations, harmful habits in their opinion worlds.

NY: What do you say, will I be able to succeed?
OY: If we sit crooked and talk crookedly; humans are going to be in trouble due to you!

NY: Is it defamation or an assessment?
OY: No, it is a compliment! It is a character analysis! I do not think that people can resist this questioning situation of yours too much. Already, I have battered them a lot.

NY: There is something else I don't understand! Are people having fun just because I'm coming?

OY: No, just because they got older one more year! They are rejoicing my leaving, not your coming! I have tortured them a lot! 2019 has become a complete 'exam year!'

NY: The exam was test or classic?
OY: It was multiple-choice! However, the mistakes took away quite true answers!

NY: Will they rejoice like that when I'm leaving?
OY: People will kill you slowly too! Because they love killing time!

NY: It is so ironic! We die, they love it!
OY: They will wake up when they die too; let them continue playing!

NY: Look, I have started to both fear and tremble; can I come with you?
OY: No man! You can't leave before your time is up! Advice to you, do not reveal that you are scaring! Even whistle as if you are immensely relaxed!

NY: Do you have any other strategy other than stress management?
OY: Already they pass 4 months of the year by sleeping! The rest of the days depends on your crisis management!

NY: I guess you are right; If I believe, I can achieve!
OY: Yes; the base of spiritual intelligence is, the mystery of wanting! If he doesn't want to give, he wouldn't give wanting!

NY: Well, why your eyes have brimmed with tears?
OY: It is time to break up! Death has come to the universe, headache is an excuse!

Self Coaching

NY: Don't forget us! Let Twitter and Instagram continue. I like your conservation!
OY: Come on, let me go! There are 4 worlds; this world, the virtual world, the world between 4 walls (!), and now the hereafter!

NY: Your address will change!
OY: What day does Google stand for, you will find me! You will like and retweet my hot (!) stories from the hereafter!

NY: It sounds like I've read this virtual chat before!
OY: It is dejavu! Carpe diem, what else I can say!

Ukey.ilet.in
VIRTUAL CHAT WITH NEW YEAR!

New Year (NY): Hello!
You: Hello new year, I hope you welcome!?

New Year: I couldn't come pretty nice! Still, hope is the poor's bread!
You: Does hope to feed you?

NY: What else is left to those who has lost his hope?
You: You are also doing philosophy like the old year!

NY: How was the old year?
You: They say you shouldn't talk badly behind the one who has gone, but we know him as bad! You talk about yourself; we wonder how it will be with you?

NY: Don't you follow the horoscopes? The previous year has been a year that sharp bends have revolved in every sense! The extraordinary 7-year burden on Aries has been removed! There is another zodiac sign that has fone through a harsh 7-year displacement! The stars do not move in vain, do not neglect following the above!
You: We can't see our future!

NY: Neglect neither the above nor the ground! The stone-ground, star-cloud will meld to each other!
You: You say that you will budge the stones in the world!
NY: New year means; innovation!
You: In short, it is innovation!

NY: Let go of the fantasy statements! Do not neglect the world by living in a tusk world like useless social scientists!

Self Coaching

You: The complicated thing is not science, the mind of scientists I guess!

NY: Your statement is true but it does not solve any problem!
You: Are you afraid of people?

NY: No, no comment!
You: It is written on social media that you have taken coaching support from the old year about how to deal with us?

NY: The ground has ears, social media has a keyboard; everyone makes up something!
You: I couldn't get a clear answer!

NY: It is a professional secret; let it stay with me!
You: Expert, let me give you a secret about people and it stay between us; there is no secret concept in the world!

NY: The old year said when he was leaving, he was right; my stress level has started to increase!
You: Zero stress is death, man!

NY: In short, it is the situation of me after 365 days!
You: How short your life is!

NY: How long is your lifetime?
You: It is a secret!

NY: The thing you don't know can't be a secret, also the thing you know too!
You: We have exceeded the 50th mile here! The concept of agedness has been changing too and the age average has been increasing to 75!

Ukey.ilet.in

NY: These are scientific illusions and film fantasies! The poet said "The age is thirty-five, it makes half of the road"; with the hope of living 70 years, but in the 46 the death comes!
You: Heaven forbid, I already exceeded! You've started to demoralizing me!

NY: The one who agrees to the faith has less sadness!
You: Humans make a plan, the destiny smiles!

NY: Plan is nothing; planning is everything!
You: However, humans wonder what will be in the destiny plan!

NY: Little time left, be patient! *"When I was little, my nanny says: The most have gone, the little has stayed. I grew up, I got older, the most went, the little stayed... Hit the digger to the mountain Ferhat, the most went, the little stayed..."*
You: There are too many leavers, the one who doesn't go doesn't leave; by saying of the people who are light-hearted get well, the sorrow will not pass, the fire burns the place where it falls!

NY: I understand your longing and it will finish one day! *"This hometown that reaches out like a mare from the Farther Asia to the Mediterranean by coming gallop is ours... Living only and freely like a tree and brotherly like a forest, this longing is ours..."*
You: Since everyone that comes will go, the important thing is to live freely and honoured in this world and like Baki said, remaining deathless in the canopy as a pleasant sound. That's the thing.

C. INDIVIDUAL CHECK-UP

COACHING TO YOURSELF!

Be yourself, be the coach of yourself! Give value, spend time, discover, make coaching to yourself in our digital era that the access to all information has become easier a lot! How? Think and start, I will only make convoy to you! Come on!

As being today's modern human, actually, you don't have an information problem. You know but you cannot apply what you know. Your biggest deficiency is not reflecting what you know to your behaviours...

Your duty is, to transfer what you know to your life with action and to make this a continuous situation. The easier to access to the information, the more difficult is it to discover the usable upper information that can change your behaviours?

Why does your information not reflect your behaviours, to applications? Maybe you are known a lot, but are your application talent and your management skills equivalent to what you know? The things that you have ascribed meaning more than adequate and supposed that they are information, actually can be only a pile of information?

Would you be offended if I told you "mindfully talkative" while living under the information bombardment? You are in an information bombardment place that is very extreme and you can't see the upper information that you actually should use. You think that every information is necessary! Actually, right now you should start an information diet! Like a human who is overweight makes diet, you should make an information diet for a more healthy and peaceful life as bein a person lives under the extreme information bombardment too!

Develop Your Self-Coaching Perfections

You are special! You have different talents and skills! You should not be a creature that is passive and stays on a second degree with these features. Although you know that you do not have the desired activism in your life and you feel sad. Do you want to find a solution to this problem? What are the factors that reduce your effectiveness? What kind of solutions can you reach by making self-coaching? Are you ready to examine it from different perspectives?

You should be a part of solutions, not the problems! You have hats more than one! You have many hats in your life like mother-father, manager-directed, educator-educated. Every of your hat means different responsibilities, different responsibilities mean different problems! While making self-coaching, your job style should always be indexed to search for solutions. You should aspire to gain this perfection and make your environment to gain.

You have an endless problem source: Your perspectives about topics like communication and management with your shareholders. You experience different troubles due to work. "How can you manage these problems?" confront you as being one of the basic questions. Your aim should be moving consciously in the management of yourself in the light of basic management concepts. Rather than the question "how?", ask the question "why?"! Because this perspective is the password of self-coaching! After entering from the door that is opened with this key, you will have reached the synergy station with the ways like process depends on planning, performance, motivation, and communication management!

You need energy filling, right? Stop by to the Synergy Station and store energy from 5 filling points:
1. Understand yourself!
2. Understand others!
3. Adapt!
4. Take action!
5. Display trustworthy behaviour!

"Can I be a Self-Coach?

The coaching profession has rules like every profession has too. If you behave appropriately for coaching, why not? The question "Do I have basic skills for self-coaching?" is the suitability questioning. Only your theoretical information is not enough for self-coaching!

One of the powerful questions is the question "can self-coaching be made?" Due to the statement "The one who demands, will find", you can't make self-coaching if you don't demand! It is necessary to jerk yourself and create awareness with the ways that we have coded as disruptive extraordinary questions pass as powerful questions in the professional standards. You will need to disruptive questions to concentrate.

One of the concepts that create the frame should be your environment and especially your family. We observe the family factors all the time as being one of the basic reasons for the conflict in the education sector. Parents' efforts to reach their own dreams draw attention when choosing a profession that is not suitable for the student's skills.

It is hard to live a life whose dream belongs to someone else. This dictation effort is between the reasons for a midlife crisis, especially rapid and radical skiddings are experienced. Such fundamental questions, which reduces the effectiveness of the company's human resources, should be addressed and reconstructed within the education system- not the educational structure. The education structure is bureaucratic and each bureaucratic structure does not cause healthy institutionalism. So, we say by making irony: "Education system has 2 missings; education and system!"

In order to create a self-coaching system, you need to examine the factors that are related to 'strategic management'. While organizing individual factors, on the other hand, the external factors are compelling you, maybe you may experience troubles that are not caused by you in an unplanned period. You should try to overcome the problems by individual reorganizations in the controllable periods of the problems, if not enough, by going to change engineering in times of crisis. Turning problems to opportunity require ability. Rather than solving a problem, turning a problem into an opportunity is the ideal thing.

"What is the Aim of the Self-Coaching Meeting?

How a successful self-coaching meeting is?"You should make a meeting with yourself! You should fulfil the inner of the concepts meaningfully like easing the learning, motivating the success. The concept of awareness is indispensable for the coaching profession. Self-knowledge, changing behaviour, success agreement with yourself, motivation-achievement-ability are the other concepts of the wheel and frame.

'Socrates' Triple Filter Test'

This test detects the borders of your information sources in the self-coaching: "If the word that you will say is not true, do not say, if it is not good, do not say, if it is not useful, do not say!" Do

Self Coaching

not keep busy yourself with the words that do not pass from this filter. The Socrates Filter can create an important perspective for you in the name of preventing information dirtiness and making an information diet.

WHAT IS SELF-COACHING?

Let's open the question with questions: What is not self-coaching? Are coaching and mentorship the same concepts? What are the fundamental coaching perfections? How is a self-coaching meeting? What is your self-coaching style? How do you make self-career coaching?

You will provide support to yourself in self-coaching. You will be careful about reaching better performance. For this, you will make meeting sessions with yourself in the name of serving solution tools!

'Self-coach does not have the answers beforehand!' Because the concepts like the problem, talent, need, aim are full of uncertainties. You need to see yourself as an honourable being, who is at the centre and subject of the event, develop a strategy that suits you by giving value to yourself. You will not educate yourself, not bend; you will make self-coaching.

'Self-Coach tries to find the solution on its own!' Since we experience trouble, you have the most ideal solution. Your all effort must be on developing the ability to think and to create alternatives. If you are at the Y or especially Z generation, your ability to make self-coaching will be more.

'Self-Coaching provides the formation of awareness!' What is awareness formation? It is the ability to create the ability to recognize the traits you have, the strengths and the pros and the weaknesses, environmental opportunities, and threats. Self-Coaching is a support service that helps the individual find the solution on their own.

Self Coaching

'Self-Coach devotes itself to the process!' If you live in a country success indexed, commitment requires this even working process-preferred is hard. In a country that most of live outcome-indexed, being process-preferred can be a nice opportunity door in the name of creating a difference. No matter how many pessimists you are at the beginning; if you think solution-preferred rather than problem detection, you can get underway to hope flood.

Do not be the illiterate with educated! Knowledge is something but not everything. You should comment, handle the knowledge, and turn it an upper knowledge. The educated illiterates can't do this. If you have the ability of awareness management, you can do it. Exposition, debate, negotiation, adding deepness to the topic with the question and exclamation points, and touching to the life want to labour.

You Intended to Coaching

You pretend to like reading, the writer pretends like writing!

You pretend like listening, they pretend like telling...

You pretend like school is finishing, they pretend like giving a diploma...

You pretend like a searching job, they pretend like giving a job...

You pretend like working, they pretend like paying...

You pretend like marrying, pretend like making career, pretend like being retired when its day comes...

Life ranges like that... One day your door is knocked carefully!

Don't live pretend like!

The one who comes doesn't pretend like coming, doesn't pretend like doing the thing he will do, doesn't bestow a privilege upon, makes his duty carefully and goes! Right here, before experiencing the fatal end, come to today again by going to the back in the time machine and restart living the moment! Condense your energy today!

Someone in depression went to the psychologist:
– Tell me about your goals?
– I am searching for myself!
– What kind of person do you want to be when you find yourself?
– I want to be rich like my boss!
– Okay, what else?
– I want to live in a villa like my boss!
– What else?
– I want to get in a lux car like my boss! When the statements like that continue, the expert cannot resist:
– " You do not search yourself, you search your boss!"

Every searcher cannot find but if you want to find, you have to search!

As being our day's modern human, one of the fundamental problems of you are your body and spirit live different worlds, right? Without recognizing your wish and necessities, you live dual in the different worlds. There are lots of people around you who are tired, daunted, sick, demotivated, broken-concentration, reproach all time, and complain! Look carefully at your environment, what is the difference between the one makes his profession with love and pretends like making? You should be the first passenger foremost of the journey of this being qualified! Then, you can say "I intend to be a coach to myself."

"The first key" is the intention!

Self Coaching

Although the first function of management passes as planning in the books, there is an intention that precedes before it and is a prerequisite. The one whose intention is broken, what happens even if his business plan is good! You have to intend to looking over your intention. If you don't start to business by fastening the first button rightly, being rinsed in the intention, it is in vain!

THE MEETING OF THE COACH WITH HIMSELF!

The outside of fantasy concepts can be nice, but there is always a risk like draining its inner till it reaches to you. If your talent of making analysis, the courage of commenting, your internalisation is not enough, the risk of simply pursuing self-confidence and moving away from self-esteem will be inevitable as being a passive individual that fulfils the requirements of the rote learning system. You need to challenge across to this risk, breaking the mould and asking powerful questions!

You need to not making the same things that are made all the time, walking to back if it is necessary in order to extinguish the flatness! If it is necessary, you need to run by hopping, but you should not do the same things all the time- same things all the time- same things all the time--same things all the time (look, you've even started to get bored while reading these repetition statements)! If you run on the same road all the time, if you are surprised when you come to the same dead-end all the time, this means the song "the same chorus all the time" is your favourite! Before searching the problem around you, you need to making a discovery to inset and making a meeting with yourself.

The Coaching Hat...

Confusing your coaching hat with your other hats and getting dragged into a role conflict can be seen as your biggest disadvantage. You are in private with yourself while making self-coaching since in your other social roles the active being is generally you, the passive being is your interlocutor! You are free to make the wrong thing you want! You need the applications that put yourself responsibility as much as possible. The actual thing is making a plan by yourself, being organized, and taking

Self Coaching

responsibilities. "The important thing is what I understand, not what you told me!" Think simple appropriate to your talents and apply, not new information, different ways, setting goals all the time. The more you become an individual that can manage yourself, the pleasure parameter will increase that you will take from your life.

Positioning yourself at the centre of the business cannot often be provided due to the bigoted education structure that resists to the necessities of the era. The dominant characters at the social places are general managers, teachers, mother-father. A person who makes his/her job by huffing and puffing can't be a talent explorer! Country human sources are already being wasted, you have the responsibility of providing a positive contribution to your own life. Even being a person, you have the obligation of looking at yourself as being a value, not being a source. Don't make Headship of Human Values, be a morale coach!

The education structure even does not need an amulet! There are too musty education applications that will not be covered! An education system that is appropriate to the necessities of the era, that reached to the tranquillity helps growing more qualified human values. This is a problem that can be solved by walking away from the understanding of 'abitur'. Become a real student!

As you often observe, some people are successful in school life but have serious distortions in university and social life. It is the situation of being an interlocutor to suffering for a lifetime, wrong department choice, and fronting to the wrong profession! He asks when he succeeded in the department: "Why did I come to this department?" He asks when he finishes: "What will happen to me?" He asks when he has a job: "This job is not appropriate to me!" The person who does not examine the reason for existence at first, questions and blames everything else. You need to self-coaching!

Advice For Coaching...

Human-*priority coaching*: Your coaching style should aim for managing yourself as being a human. You will consider valuable as an honourable person and you will accept people around you in their own positions regardless of their religion, language, belief, belonging.

Y Paradigm Coaching

You need to develop a business style with a priority perspective of Y theory for sympathetic and empathetic coaching. Show active patience, be constantly on the move by challenging to every problem!

Stop and think in the name of having active coaching abilities

Are things for you to live better, or, do you exist to get things done better? Do you have to do the things right, or do you have to do the right things? I am like hearing that you say 'The best is to make the right things in the right way'! A person who has a leading spirit remains on the lives he has touched! Touch yourself! If you want to leave a permanent mark, if you want to stay as a pleasant sound on the canopy, take the heart hammer to your hands and start clicking! Even you have problems, you should be able to mount yourself to social life! The manager tries to do things properly. As for that, the leader makes the right things! The

Self Coaching

self-coach is not a manager, it is a leading candidate! What about you?

YOUR STYLE!

Let's interpret the concept of management skills and leadership in terms of self-coaching:

Technical Skill: The practical skill that you will need to get a job done.

Communication Skill: Your skill to transfer the existing information verbally and non-verbally.

Human Relations Skill: Your skill to work in harmony with the interlocutor and understand your environment.

Analytical Skill: Your ability to approachability in solving problems logically, scientifically, analytically.

Decision-Making Skill: The skill of choosing the most appropriate decision between alternatives at the most appropriate time.

Conceptual Skill: Your ability to handle problems of a complex structure holistically.

Human is on the basis of education. Every word about you, every behaviour is actually subjective. You are not an objective creature. You are not a rational creature. You act more with your feelings. Do not forget mind-heart balance. People are busier with reflecting negative situations to their environment by acting with their emotions. So, modern people ring busy all the time! The speed of your eating is the speed of taking decisions! The speed of walking is the speed of talking! The average will reveal the management skills of your features too. Do not force a lot, live slow!

If you live in a country that the one wakes up early is the manager, your job is hard! If you live in a country where it is more important to who you know than what you know, your job is hard! The question 'Isn't making self-coaching would be hard if my features are not available?' will come to the mind. If you don't have leadership features enough, it will provide psychological relief by aiming to be a great player of a team rather than getting caught too complex. None of us is perfect, but you are special!

You've started to revive your roles in social life with your personality that settle after adolescence and formed due to inborn characteristics and environmental effects. You will have to go behaviour changes without defecting the excuses like "I am not planned, I am untidy" by making habit-changing exercises. Even if you are fifty, you need to try canalizing a negative behaviour to positive by making behaviour changing exercises.

You have a different role at the stage of life like every individual. The leading role in which the eyes are on you on the stage is coaching to yourself. Ask this question: "If the aim is active coaching, can coaching be more implemented through education leadership or education management?" If your answer is option a, the following question will be this: "How can I make education leadership more effective?" Your actual aim is being active, not success!

Your successes are temporary. Effort and patience are enough to be successful. You focus and reach the target by trial and error. Do not fall the mistake of fallacy-trying! The target is not being successful; because you can be unsuccessful the next day by being successful today, your performance can increase or decrease. The target is; how can you do your work more effectively and how can you be more effective as being a self-coach. The activity requires consciousness and depth. In order to remain deep marks in life and add plus value, the activity should be your target.

For activity, you must essentially have 'job discipline and inner discipline.' You can match the job discipline with technical knowledge and inner discipline with motivation. Why discipline or what is discipline? The actual thing in discipline is job follow-up, not human follow-up! Why can't you provide enough job discipline despite all your opportunities? You can examine the socio-cultural dimensions of this.

Do not forget that the actual handicap is in the inner discipline and this deficiency affects the job discipline negatively. If your inner discipline is enough, you can make enough challenge with the questions related to the profession. Love for profession lies at the heart of the internal discipline. How enjoyable problem solving is while humming the tune "I love my trouble!"

One of the two wings in the activity is technic and the other one is motivation. The first one is the ability to apply theoretical information related to the business. The other one is the enthusiasm and your talent in transferring technical knowledge to life. If one of them is not enough, how long can you go with only one wing? This thing starts with a dream and a ship will not sink in the dream sea! The dream has no cost. The target is the consideration threshold that can be evolved to upper information, not pink dreams. Because empty dreams and useless information are not different than waste! You aspire to business and interior architecture, not an information porter!

THE APPLICATION: COACHING PARAMETER

Can you do self-coaching? What is your perfection level? Apply the Self-Coaching Test to yourself and detect your coaching parameter…

The Parameter of Understanding Yourself

The discovery journey into one's inner world and meeting with himself continues for a long time. Yunus Emre says "There is an I inside me inner than myself." As a coach, what is your parameter of understanding yourself out of 100?

The Parameter of Perception

The effort of understanding myself, which is a prerequisite, will provide support to the parameter of perception from your environment. The one who discovers yourself will be in a more accurate communication with his environment. As a coach, what is your parameter of perception out of 100?

The Empathy Parameter

How much can you think by putting yourself in the shoes of those around you? Even if you can't be empathetic, you can't be sympathetic. If you can thinking sessions by putting yourself in the shoes of others, you can understand the others. As a coach, what is your empathy parameter out of 100?

The Adaptation Parameter

What is harmony? What do you understand from harmony? You are not very compatible with the definition of harmony! When we say a harmonious person, is a docile person rousing who has a mouth-no language in your mind or a different type that can express himself? The actual powerful questions are these: Harmony with what? Harmony with who? For example, what comes to your mind when we say loyal staff, obedient children? Obedience to what? Loyalty to what? Is the child who never examines you loyal or the child who can argue with questions, make comments, object to you, and even can touch the horizon line of you is more loyal? The provision of the coach about this topic is: "The harmony occurs to a meaningful mission and rich vision, not to a person, manager, bureaucratic structure, etc.!" As a self-coach, -appropriate to the provision- what is your adaptation parameter out of 100?

The Taking Action Parameter

Now that the philosophical dimension of the event has been completed, it means that the time of action has come. I wonder how much is your active patience parameter. You can't make self-coaching by sitting, grunting, and reproaching! You will love your trouble, smile at your problems, and turn them into opportunities. For example, a colleague that you can't get on well might be an opportunity for you! At least what does it bring you? The mitzvah (good deed) of patience! It is actually a gşft pack that has been sent to you in order to develop your management skills. You will accept him like that and be patient with you since your break up. Thank goodness when you break up! The effect is the power of remaining a mark. Are you aware of how a mark you will leave behind, oh coach? Do you have any intention of consciousness management? How many times have you knocked on the door of awareness management? As a self-coach, what is your taking action parameter out of 100?

Evaluation

Self Coaching

Add up your points, determine the parameter of coaching by diving to 5. Compare and evaluate the maximum score of 500 with your own score:

Up to 100: You are too weak
(You need to the studies that will develop your coaching skills urgently and seriously.)

Up to 200: You are weak
(You need to the studies that will develop your coaching skills urgently.)

Up to 300: You are at an intermediate level
(You can experience occupational problems later in life.)

Up to 400: You are at a good level
(You can be better.)

Between 400-500: You are at such a good level
(You should keep improving by saying 'Not what I've become, what will I be?)

IT IS CONSCIOUSNESS MANAGEMENT, NOT LYNCH!

In front of a large rock, the sculptor is carving the rock, his grandchild is watching. After a while, a work that is art wonder occurs. –Grandma, how did this work of art occur? –My son, actually I did not anything. This phantom has already been in the stone, I just threw the useless parts of stone! If you make consciousness management, disable the useless parts on yourself, reveal your talents, do not stoop, and bend while saying I am having education; don't make shaved your character! Now that you live in the changing era, you need to manage the change and be flexible. If you have quite strict rules, this means actually your self-confidence is low. If you have peace of mind, your self-confidence is higher.

Management is a science but first of all and especially it is a work of art; an ability, an application. In the name of being an active person, analyze tools like planning, organizing, managing, and supervision. Search the concepts like planning tool, mission, vision, strategic plan. In order to make active leadership, improve your ability to be organized. As you bring together the concepts of leadership, motivation, communication, and supervision in your life in a meaningful way, your individual effectiveness will increase. The question "Is my lifestyle, way of life is appropriate to my individual characteristics, right?" ask yourself.

You need to open the blocked veins by making the right interferences at the right time in terms of personality. If you haven't done this reorganization study on time, the last resort is you have to obliged to reconstruction activity over again by going to change engineering. Be careful! If you haven't done all of this enough and if the damage is done, your brain death happens. This is your failure. In order to not experience Rigor Mortis, think proactively and, do not neglect yourself before being helpless.

Your inborn characteristics are so important for leadership. If you want to do manservant leadership, you need to make a "horizontal revolution"! In a world, that whole social life yields to vertical hierarchical and bureaucratic structure, even the concept of manservant leadership look weird, but you should not be surprised that it will become one of the popular concepts that will be needed again in the world of future.

Make a journey of examining life in order to be a conscious person with the question "why?", not "how?"! Without having enough knowledge of what you do, as a person who has not improved conscious management, you wager the future of your interlocutors by carving. How about living more consciously in order to be able to make conscious management, not lynch?

Your Motivation!

Do you have enough motivation to read this article? Motivation but how? How will you provide motivation under environmental pressure? Is the priority yourself or your environment in motivation? How will you provide auto-motivation? How will you manage the problems? Motivation but how? You have different responsibilities that you should follow in the work-flow on your agenda. You have different troubles in your job and private life. How will you provide motivation under this pressure? Is the priority here your own motivation or the motivation of your interlocutors? If you don't examine yourself, you can't shake your interlocutors!

How will you provide auto-motivation? It is not possible to be happy all the time but you constantly play different roles at the stage due to your different responsibilities. Instead of complaining about your troubles, the necessity of the philosophy 'I love my trouble', you need to achieve being able to smile to your environment in some way. Of course, this is not easy, it is difficult but not impossible, just it will take some time!

Motivation is dangerous when there is no morality. Have a motivation target that is appropriate to ethics. If the motivation is not enough, your capacity does not occur. If your capacity does not occur, your ability will not improve. Do not understand motivation as a desire for making a job. Motivation is; your desire for making a job, your starting decision, your determination to continue and will of getting a result. Your determination to review the result and continue the event again will be your sustainable motivation. If you do not look to the motivation concept with the logic of an inclusive wholesale package program like that, you always deal with the jobs in a retail way and live a shattered life. How will you manage the problems? A nice question to this question: "Are your management abilities enough?" Making your role at social life by wanting is different, pretending like doing is different. Do not pass by saying "When God does not give, what else can I do!" You must have something to do absolutely; search and find!

You can be motivated to a certain extent with different motivation techniques in life. So, it is ideal to be in the right places with the right people at the right times. Provided that you are right too! As for the curves; do not waste time with them because you can't fix the curve bananas! You look to fix your own missings. Forget the defending mechanisms like "I wish I had a well-paid job…"! Think about what your profession will take from your life and environment, and the cost of your profession, which is paid but not loved!

You can't take benefit from the motivation techniques with, however, let's say you have taken, you can't get over the midlife crisis! Your life movie finishes in a minute! After that, you already

Self Coaching
will not need motivation! If you read the article till here, it means that you've taken the first motivation tablet to your body! May your light and energy abundance, not your soil!

CONSUME THE BURNOUT SYNDROME!

When you have burnout syndrome, you both make sad yourself and your interlocutors. You live your own life story like everyone. So, don't you have to focus on handicaps in your life and your weaknesses?

What are the symptoms of burnout syndrome in general? You need to pay attention to the physical and emotional signs of the syndrome. You should take into account physical signs like tiredness, fatigue, cold, and insomnia.

Forgetfulness is the most important problem for you. There is also information in old sources about this. You can do several exercises such as memorization, puzzle-solving, and writing to remove forgetfulness. Especially you should do these and similar exercises on time so that you do not experience big problems in middle and old ages.

Loss of interest aimed at the environment is one other symptom of burnout syndrome. The concepts like "Well, what am I doing here now?", "Why did I come here?" keep busy your mind all the time.

Do not delay, do it right now!

Delaying the jobs, seeing yourself as unsuccessful, postponing the communication are the other symptoms. If you go to your appointments late or you do not go without a reason, you should pay attention to this point!

What should you do?

Self Coaching

You should also review your inner motivation sources not only the external ones. You should put your life the concept of Spiritual Quotient (SQ) not only Intelligence Quotient (IQ), Emotional Quotient (EQ). I write useful topics like inner motivation tools and spiritual intelligence for you in this book! If you have burnout syndrome, you can use a UKEY ebook dragee!

YOUR INNER MOTIVATION SOURCES

You run after the external motivation tools with the anxiety of work-food-wife in general. You need to direct your attention to inner motivation tools like yourself, your life philosophy, individual mission, and vision in some way. Listen to the wonderful determination of Russian scientist who studies the brain and discover yourself: If we load 10 new information to our brain, which has 1400 kg weight, every second up to the age of 70 we can fill much less than half of our memory capacity!" Do not pretend like today's mind-boggling person and after some occupation do not say "I can't pick up anymore"! Do not forget that the actual reason for this is fatigue. Remember that fatigue is more than psychologic, not psychologic; you can get over it with suggestions and active resting. You have a perfect capacity like that. Can you have a source better than this for motivation? You carry this brain on your head every day! Respect yourself and delete lack of self-confidence from the black book! Even write off the black book from your life and open white pages on a white book! If you recognize this feature of you in real meaning, maybe you will experience self-confidence burst!

Apart from this enormous capacity of the brain, you have sensitive eyes that can see the light of a candle far from 25-30 km in the darkness of night! If you spend an estimated 70 million dollars to make these eyes with today's technology, you still cannot make an organ equivalent to these eyes! How painful that you cannot see the future with these eyes in daylight! What problem cannot you solve when you load the heart and spiritual intelligence into your life after the brain and eye? If your problems cannot be solved, it means that you are looking at your problems often negative and inverse perspective from the blind spot of your potential.

Read the English letters above loud and fast!:

"THEGODISNOWHERE"

What did you perceive at first glance?
God Is Nowhere!
God Is Now Here!
God Is Now Where!

Which one? How did you read? If your attention has focused on the "No statement" first, it is time to change the perspective of No as Now right now! If it is not now, when?

How meaningful is the message on a dirty car: "The dirty one is your glances!" When you look out of the window; you can see the dirt on the window too, the amazing view exists behind the window too! The glance is yours!

The Motive of Love

In the interesting experiment that Harlow made on baby monkeys (1962-1965) the motive of love is emphasized as an unlearned inner motive. The aim is to determine whether baby monkeys attach to their mothers solely because they provide food and whether affection for the mother depends only on physiological motives. Two types of mother-like mannequin monkeys were used; the first was from wire, the second was from cotton fabric on wood. There were milk bottles that baby monkeys can suck milk as much as they want behind the mother from the wire. The mother from cotton was representing a mother that is warm, soft, patience, never gets angry and, stays with them but has not a milk bottle. The result is; it was seen that the baby monkeys had preferred the mother from the cotton whether it has milk source or not. Except for the time when they are hungry, their attention is being in a place that can be hugged rather than being near to milk. So that they attached to the mother from the cotton and react as if it was a real mother. For example, when a scaring thing was seen, they defected to the mother from the cotton. It has been determined that babies who are given to institutions for various reasons show healthy growth and living (speaking, walking on time, etc.) according to the degree of the warm and close attention they receive in these institutions. All these results show the existence of an unlearned motive in living things, especially in the human species. " Use your love motive a little bit on yourself!

In the past, people say while leaving the house "my lady, if you are depressed, do not cook, we can't eat that food!" You have to aspire to positive of this life that passes in pursuit of livelihood! You will work a lot, be patient to the result. Your sources are enough in life, don't worry! The limitless thing is your wishes and desires. For example, you want not to die and live eternally. This is your desire. This cannot be prevented. But your needs are limited! You need to recognize that these are separate from each other.

What will you aspire to? You try to aspire to peace! Your job and environment, all of them are a tool for you to be more peaceful. But if your tools have replaced to your targets, you can't search peace there. Your stress factor, tensions, anger, and conflicts peak there. So, sessions like conflict management, stress management, motivation problems are quite popular! But you see, nothing much changes in your life. Why? Because you have serious troubles in the fundamental issues. You should live far from self-esteem! "If you want to be happy, know your limits, accept them" and challenge the problems with your existing abilities! Turn to the inside, be open!

YOUR SPIRITUAL INTELLIGENCE

As an individual, you live as a being that goes back and forth at the plus and minus points but always seeks balance. You see, only your intelligence parameter (IQ) is not enough in getting over the problems. Because as an intelligent person but with low concentration, you may not be quite patient with problems. As a generation that 'I have my iPhone on my hands, do I care about the world', it is quite normal to experience low motivation and loss of concentration a lot!

Emotional Quotation (EQ) alone is not enough to overcome problems. You should give support to IQ and EQ with your spiritual intelligence (SQ). The Spiritual Quotation says that devote yourself to the process, not to result! The result is not your job. You can't solve the problem with the only IQ; your ego swells. You can't solve it with the only heart; there will be offences. If you include your spiritual intelligence, spiritual values, psychological status, and sociological facts into the event, you will have the chance to go over the problems more holistically with the logic of a package program.

No matter how much you make the program as an individual, no matter how much your intelligence and heart you put into the work, you will still not be able to overcome the problems in life alone! You should not take wrong decisions by gushing and being caught up in the winds of personal development like a person has "unlimited power" with false emphasis. You mean something to those around you. Even if you are a genius, the era of genius is over today; the period is the period of the common mind. If you can be part of a meaningful whole, if you can add value to a team, you make sense for fertility management.

Self Coaching

In our day, which is a polished image era, your effort to polishing your ego does not decelerate all on the brink of you often experience, unfortunately! Actually, this does not get along with your cultural codes, not all that. This type of approach may be working more in the West because of the social lives of these societies, these concepts have a starting point and meaningful response. It can be working since individualism is in the foreground but in the geographics that are scudded in the chaos, there is more need for the collective consciousness.

While aborigines are controlling the maturation of potatoes under the ground with mental power, won't you be able to control the problems above the ground? While a local that has been sentenced to kill himself by being excluded from the group is dying by giving himself suggestion, won't you be able to throw your negative behaviours from yourself? While items can be moved with mental power without being touched, won't you be able to prompt you and your environment with your mental intelligence? As long as you want! Are you aware of your power of believing and are you sure about what you want? Can be the things that you cannot achieve in life would not be the things you want without wanting? It is not said in vain "The believers, believe"! Because only with a real believe you can challenge the problems of the world!

One of the most locked points of motivation is; setting powerful goals by reviewing your targets when the moment that your behaviours start to weaken! If your targets are powerful, your behaviours will become a meaningful and lively situation. Why do you want to? Do you have strong reasons?

You can't climb the success stairs by whistling with hands in your pockets! You will reach your targets by wanting till the end; insistently, without giving up, knowing how to get up even if you fall. "If you knew God properly, the mountains would move with your prays." If you can't move, who's the fault? Are you determined to wanting till its end with emotion power and persistence power? If you haven't reached the desired result despite all of your efforts, will you be able to want? Is your persuasion power enough?

Let me summarize you the concept of spiritual intelligence by transferring a short part of my own coach's life: He lived at peace with himself by saying that "I do my best" although he could not win the university for 4 years, he did not give up from effort journey like a patience hero and at the end, he won department of art with his special talent, he finished and did his profession in Ankara and Istanbul with love. When his career journey finishes with 1999 Turkey Marmara Earthquake at the age of 33, he had asked his last question that shook me: *"What will your line be in this world where the scene of powerful ones is experienced?"*

Self Coaching

YOUR COMMUNICATION ACCIDENTS

Zero communication?

Is there zero communication? How will you provide the quality in communication? Are you from the ones with whom we can't communicate? How will you make communication more effective? How much does a smile cost? There is no zero communication, there is negative communication. When you don't give a promise to your interlocutor when he takes your right to sharing information from you, you are a clever distinguished personality, the interlocutor is a passive creature that is dependant on information! You are active, your interlocutor is passive, the issue has been done, the communication has been cut. Then you are trying to direct your interlocutor to the target with different methods. You have made all intelligence types failure, bare techniques have remained away.

Body Language

What is the sense of your around related to you? How is your image? If it is positive, you are with advantage, what will you do if it is negative? You can start the work by reviewing your body language. How much can you improve your body language by reading bad translation books, by taking sessions from an educator whose own body language is negative? You need to develop a meaningful body language with an interpretative understanding and look for ways to communicate more effectively so that your communication accidents will decrease.

There are different behaviour types in different cultures. For example, a thing that will be given to the interlocutor is extended with both hands because giving it with one hand is accepted as impoliteness! Especially, it is never given with the left hand which is accepted as dirty! Understanding the behaviours of your interlocutors' behaviours from different cultures depends on your knowledge and emotional intelligence. If you don't show respect to different cultures and behaviour types including the cultural mosaic in your country, you can't see respect!

Difficult Person Management

Difficult people tire you, right? The difficult person loves painting into a corner to his interlocutors. Actually, every problem has a solution type. Let's list the general determinations of psychiatrists about difficult person management: Talking without listening, not giving oneself to what is said, thinking yourself as if too enough, transferring his knowledge hardly, not being able to list his priorities, not being able to make time management, moving too slow by thinking slowly, the desire of purifying oneself, not being able to make empathy.

Knowing yourself is pretty important. You can help from the different character analyses like Hippocrates' 4 personality types. There are so many sources from classic books such as Marifetname to new books such as Elfabe that interpret palm lines, the important thing is to be able to manage information.

Your Communication Map

Review your own behaviours! Face with your problems! Look whether there is a change or not! Try to turn the differences to advantage! If even these approaches do not work, do not be offended to the world!

Your courage of coming down to problem but do not cut trying! Whatever you do, achieve the behaviour change.

Self Coaching

SELF-CONSCIOUSNESS PRACTICE

"Science is to know, science is to know yourself. If you don't know yourself, this is how reading." The precondition of being able to make consciousness management passes from making self-consciousness. Are you aware of yourself? Do you know your features enough as a person? How about starting the study of self-consciousness study right now with a short practice?

Practice
Write your determinations on the following 6 topics:

• What are your psychological barriers?
....

• What are your individual characteristics?
....

• What are your motivation tools?
....

• Write a sentence that expresses your philosophy of life:
....
(For example: "The destiny of a person finds the person, and the person should seek the peace!")

• Write a sentence that expresses your mission:
....
(For example: "I try to make people look to life with exclamation!")

• Write a sentence that expresses your vision:
....

Self Coaching

(For example: "No matter how original you think; if your horizon is not extended, the things that you can do are the limits of your village !")

Score yourself out of 100 for each of the topics below:

- Your planning ability:
- Your leadership succeed:
- Your profession love:
- Your sense of corporate belonging:
- Your parameter of professional commitment:

Add up the points. Find your awareness average by dividing the sum to 5. Compare and evaluate your own score with the maximum awareness score of 500:

Up to 100: Very weak
(You have a very urgent and serious need for awareness studies.)

Up to 200: Weak
(You urgently need awareness programs.)

Up to 300: Medium
(You may experience occupational problems later in life.)

Until 400: Good
(You can be better.)

Between 400-500: Very good
(Keep improving by saying "What will I be, not what I am?")

This application is an example of awareness management that has been developed specifically with an interpretative and subjective perspective.

INDIVIDUAL SWOT PRACTICE

Self Coaching

This analysis, whose original name is SWOT (Strengths, Weakness, Opportunities, Threats) enables detecting the important factors that affect our performance significantly and detecting the things that will be done toward these. It is not easy to clearly identify the positive and negative strategic issues that affect us in the daily rush of life.

Individual SWOT Analysis

You need to SWOT analysis in terms of an individual with inner and external factors and with a close and far perspective. Do not neglect the effort of knowing yourself better in terms of opportunities, superior aspects, threats, and weaknesses by making a practical analysis with the logic of strategic planning.

How can I make my own analysis as an individual?

What opportunities do I have as an individual? What are my superiorities as an individual? What are the factors that threat me as an individual? What are my weaknesses as an individual? The point you will be careful at here is that two of these titles (S, W) are close, and two are (O, T) distant factors. It is important to determine the map of the act after the determinations you will make under 4 headings as items.

List the effective factors in 4 headings by applying the SWOT analysis to yourself. Then, create an action plan about how to solve the problems and how to evaluate the positive issues by starting off from these items.

IDEAL SELF-COACHING

Ruin the Comfort

Do the unmade things, try the untested things, delete the excuses, produce skills, smile to a new life, start a new career. Ruin the comfort of your life with "rebellion morality" and walk! They say "don't!" in unison! Don't live for them say! Do, try, delete, produce, smile, start, ruin, walk. Come on…

"That head" is so bigot in the issues that it thinks as a right that it does not desire to examine and thinking. If you say why the people whose self-confidence is low build the criticism walls too high around them. The people who do not trust themselves do not want to be criticised.

People with high self-confidence are more flexible. This type of individual live peace with themselves, do their jobs with love, add joy to the issue.

In general, people who have "somehow" occupied certain positions, since they see themselves as more competent and knowledgeable, they try to adapt their interlocutors to the system they design without paying too much attention to the needs and goals of them.

What will you do in the face of these impositions? Will you complain all the time or will you take action? Will you be a part of the solution or problem? Don't you think coming down to the problems by creating a synergy with the environment?

Today's people carry an invisible excuse bag! They have excuses that are ready to be served in case of failure. You should produce a skill, not an excuse! Every profession owner can use

Self Coaching

his/her excuse right; there is no place to excuses in the professions that directs to the society and people like; coaching, consultancy, educationist, judicature-prosecution!

What about a new life and a new career by making the unmade things, trying the untested things, deleting the excuses, producing skills? They will say "don't!" in unison! Are you ready to ruin the comfort of your life with "rebellion morality"? You come this time listen to yourself and go where your heart takes you! Come on!

Stupid Cougar Syndrome!

The smart cougar calculates while running after its prey that how much energy it will provide to him when he is caught! Let's say it is 200 units. But how much energy is used to catch the prey? 150 units. Is it worth it, yes! Run then! It runs, cannot catch it, continues running for a long time and has consumed more than 150 units of energy when he finally caught. In the stupid cougar syndrome, there is the persistence of running for a lifetime after the same goal that has become meaningless. Review your goals not to fall this syndrome!

You study university but you are not conscious! You graduate but you are not happy! Let's say that you found a job but you are not peaceful! You have been continually running after your own goals –but some of them are meaningless- for a lifetime. You experience stupid cougar syndrome and sustain it!

The way you eat yogurt may be different or even you don't like it, you may not eat! The important thing is being able to improve your own style. After all, this life is yours. But do not give up on the goodness management support efforts that will affect your life even maybe your after death!

Ukey.ilet.in

Do not pass by saying career, be careful while determining a career map. You should know that every person will be successful in at least one profession in life! Academic success isn't everything in this life. Some young people could not be successful in social life who graduated from science high school but signed to succeed stories who graduated from vocational high school. Some people signed to successes with their entrepreneurialism that did not study university.

It is a nice feeling to let others know the information you have. Be a social therapist, whatever role you play! The way to provide this support service is to be able to look at the events positively but be realistic at the same time.

Be open to continuous improvement! The number of the world has reached three now; 'this world' that is full of the problems Corona has captured, 'the other world' without end-problem and 'virtual world' that dazzles! If you don't exist in the virtual world, it is debated how effective you can be in this world. Look for the ways of using actively the world of virtual reality that has become nearly the real-world in our day. Or you may be offline for the ones who call you!

IDEAL COACH: YOURSELF

The ideal coach should not feel at the peak all the time!

The ideal coach should know being unsophisticated and being under. The office of an ideal coach cannot be a tusk castle! He especially keeps away from locating himself at the top in the vertical hierarchical structure! Ideal coaching is not making management; there are enough pretenders!

The ideal coach is a modern illiterate who committed himself to the continuous learning process!

The ideal coach wonders fundamental coaching perfections and tries to reveal his personal coaching style! In order to coach more effectively and coaching in his dream, accepts that he will not be an ideal coach without thinking hard about communication.

The ideal coach cares about knowing himself, setting goals, using his sources better. An ideal coach break the routines, idealizes, makes patience management with his leadership breezes. He has become the model of win-win to his life philosophy. The coach is flexible, the person who can stretch. If the plan is ruined, he is the person who does not demoralizes. Because, "plan is nothing, planning is everything!" for him.

The ideal coach is an idealist that serves at his home-job-food more, not the one who demands something. Coach does not produce a problem, he produces happiness!

The ideal coach improves in the dignified climate of self-esteem, far from the absurd seasons of self-esteem. When he decides to a job, he says "a people who return from the rice, her/his spoon will be broken" and goes until taking a result.

The ideal coach is the person who is locked to the process, not to the result. Ideal coach lives away from the swirl of burnout by feeding with spiritual sources like a bio-energy expert.

The ideal coach is the coach that can affect his environment positively, otherwise, he can't reap from his life.

The ideal coach aims to convert the doubt "*I don't believe I will succeed!*" to belief. He seeks the ways of converting the negative belief "*I believe I cannot succeed!*" to positive. He is the individual that reaches the peak of "*I believe I will succeed!*" between the dilemmas "*I don't believe I will succeed!*" or "*I believe I cannot succeed!*"

My Coach

If you said that I intend qualified self-coaching; before is artisanship and after is destiny work. "*The destiny of a person finds the person, and the person should seek serenity.*" Although not every seeker can find it, the ones who found are the seekers!

Are you ready to look at life with exclamation?

If you are ready; may your way be open and your work be fertile!

If you are not ready; it means that you've started your development journey by finishing this book!

Life is short, the required jobs are a lot!

Self-coaching is an essential tool to fertilise your short life!

Self Coaching

It is worth running after this ideal for a lifetime in the dream world; in order to add spirit to your spirit!

Goodbye to you…

Printed in Great Britain
by Amazon